The journey parents make

Surviving and thriving as a parent today

Marion Stroud

Text of *The Journey Parents Make* copyright © 1994 Marion Stroud
This edition copyright © 1994 CPAS

Published by **CPAS**
Athena Drive
Tachbrook Park
WARWICK
CV34 6NG

ISBN 1 8976 6011 1

First edition 1994
Cover design by Blade Communications
Text design by AD Publishing Services Ltd

Acknowledgements: Bible text is from the *Holy Bible, New International
Version*, copyright © 1973, 1978, 1984 by International Bible Society

British Library Cataloguing-in-Publication Data: a catalogue record for
this book is available from the British Library

Church Pastoral Aid Society
Registered Charity No 1007820
A company limited by guarantee

Contents

Preface

We hope that this book will be useful to you in a number of ways. The book is in two parts, and both parts have a different story to tell. This part, called *The Journey Parents Make*, helps you consider your own needs as a parent and to look at family life today. You will also gain some practical ideas on the skills you need as a parent.

The second part, printed the other way up and called *The Questions Children Ask*, helps you look at how to answer some of those difficult questions that children ask, such as: Why do we have conservation, Why am I fat, Who made God, What is AIDS? We've suggested answers to 100 questions like these, and set them in the broader context of how we talk and listen to our children.

This book is part of a larger resource called *HELP! I'm a Parent*, made up of video programmes and group discussion materials. Groups using the video can help each other work out how to deal with issues of bringing up children today.

Parents who have been to such groups seem to gain confidence as well as new insights into being a parent. Most parents seem to think that they are the only ones who have ever felt bad or down about their kids, or worried about things – what a relief to find others in the same position! If you are part of a group of parents using the video resource, you will find that there are suggestions as to which parts of the book fit into the group discussions.

Our prayer is that this book will help you in your journey as a parent, and that through it God will help you to carry out that important task to the best of your ability and with his strength and inspiration.

Marion Stroud
Penny Frank

1
All At Sea?

'God said to Noah, "... Make yourself an ark... I am going to bring floodwaters on the earth to destroy all life under the heavens... You are to bring into the ark two of all living creatures, male and female, to keep them alive with you."'

Every child knows the story of Noah. When the animals were facing extinction from a vast flood, God commanded Noah to build an ark and to save two of every kind. And so Noah started to build – with no hint of the coming rain, never mind a flood.

I think that those of us who are parents have a lot in common with Noah. After nearly twenty-nine years on the job, it appears to me that giving time and energy to creating and maintaining a family today is very much like building an ark in the middle of the desert. It can seem as if there isn't much point to it!

The Bible story tells us that Noah built the ark according to God's detailed plan. It was to be so many cubits this way and so many that way. Those of us who are struggling to nail together some sort of structure which will keep our particular family afloat don't have such a clear set of directions. The old measurements and standards, so we are told, are out, and the new ones seem to be of doubtful value. Building a family in the 1990s is definitely a voyage of discovery for all involved.

All change

'The trouble with us,' complained Sally, 'is that things never seem to be settled for more than a couple of months at a time. After Christmas life seemed so much easier with Louise sleeping through the night at last, and Peter having got over his dislike of his new teacher. But now my mother has broken her leg, which is awful for her, and it also means that she can't mind the children for me while I'm at work. But Mike is on short time working and we need my money to help with the mortgage so, before you can blink, we've got a whole new set of problems to contend with. I'm sure life wasn't so difficult when I was a kid. We seemed to jog along quietly most of the time, and the biggest upheaval I had to face was moving out of my bedroom to share with my sister when Gran came for her annual visit.'

I knew what she meant. Family life today reflects the pace of life in general, and families are like a mobile hanging in front of an open window in a stiff wind. They're in constant motion!

What is a family?

Our ideas about what a family is have changed too. In Noah's day, the word 'family' often meant a household of people who lived together. But even then it was a far cry from the nuclear family with its mother, father and two point four children, or the family unit headed by one adult that we are familiar with today. The household of the early part of the Bible would have consisted of at least:

- great-grandfather and his wife (or wives)
- his sons and their wives + any unmarried daughters
- his grandsons and their wives + dependent family workers
- the new generation of children.

This meant that a family could have as many as 50 to 100 members in total.

Living close together, so that you could care for and support one another as you made your living from the land, was the way that families operated far beyond Bible times. In fact it was the general pattern of life for the majority, up to the Industrial Revolution. And even after more people moved to the towns and cities, they still lived most of their lives within a few miles of where they were born. The word 'family' then meant grandparents, parents and children, aunts, uncles and cousins. They might not get on with one another all the time, but they were always on hand. And the various activities and concerns of this network of relationships were an inescapable part of each of their day-to-day lives.

The value of this supportive family network living close at hand hasn't changed but it is rarely how families operate today. Although we may sometimes hanker after the Christmas-card picture of several generations crammed happily around the table (in peace and harmony of course!) and feel that any other pattern of family life is a poor substitute for the 'real thing', we have to accept that for many people in the Western world, this kind of close-knit living disappeared with housemaids and horse-drawn transport. The word 'family' has come to mean something very different for those of us living in the closing years of twentieth-century Britain.

Sweeping changes in the way families live their lives began in the 1930s, and as the pace of life has speeded up since then, almost every ten years has seen a different pattern emerging.

■ The fighting family: 1930s and 1940s

During this period, men were often away from home in the armed forces, and women were working outside of the home in large numbers for the first time. Many children were evacuated from the cities for safety, and country families were suddenly enlarged by these evacuees, who weren't always welcome guests, with their very different outlook and expectations.

■ The re-formed family: 1950s
As men came back from the war and resumed their jobs, women were once more largely seen as home-makers, and for a little while the old order of things seemed as if it might be re-established. But the increase of labour-saving devices in the home, a desire for the money to buy them and a more enlightened attitude towards further education for girls, meant that this state of affairs didn't last.

■ The free-for-all family: 1960s
The 'swinging Sixties' saw a generation of young people growing up, who were often more interested in exploring their new-found freedoms than settling down to traditional family life. Even so, there was still a degree of togetherness within the family – at least they often ate together! So a family in the 1960s might be described as 'a group of related people living in the same house, whose lives are linked by the dining room table'.

■ The fractured family: 1970s and 1980s
As divorce and illegitimacy lost their tag of social disgrace, and birth control became easily available whether or not you were married, families began to fragment. 'Living together' either before or instead of marriage became commonplace, and divorce was seen as the accepted solution when a relationship didn't 'work out'. As more and more people moved in order to get jobs, wide family support and care was reduced. Even within the immediate family, communication wasn't helped by the increasingly

8

common ownership of a television, and meals on a tray in front of the 'telly' gave rise to the picture of a 70s and early 80s family as 'a group of related people living in the same house, whose lives are linked by a television set'.

■ The disintegrating family: 1990s

People, even within a family group, are living increasingly separate lives. Communication tends to be reduced to notes, written as individuals rush off to yet another commitment. Even television fails to keep us together in the same room, because each family member often has his or her own set.

Throughout the school holidays, Andy spent so much of his time at our house that I began to wonder if his mother resented his frequent absence. But when I suggested that she would be expecting him home for an evening meal, he replied blithely, 'Mum will be at work. It's a good thing I was born at the weekend or she wouldn't have been able to take the time off to have me! Dinner will be in the fridge, waiting for me to "nuke" it.'

I suspect that Andy (and many others of his generation) have the idea that 'family' today means 'a group of related people living separate lives under the same roof, linked mainly by a microwave oven'!

Facing extinction?

Families are under threat, just as all of animal life came close to extinction in the story of Noah.

Many parents want the family to survive. They *want* to build and sail their 'ark' so that they can keep family values alive and well whatever storm may buffet them.

So don't let's despair just yet, but take a look at what 'materials' we might need to gather together, so that we can start building an ark that will keep us afloat in the roughest of water!

2
Building the Ark

'God said to Noah, "Make yourself an ark of cypress wood; make rooms in it and coat it with pitch inside and out. This is how you are to build it... make a roof for it... put a door in the side of the ark and make lower, middle and upper decks..."'.

Discovering
the tools and materials

The Bible story does not describe the day-by-day job of building the ark, nor the tools Noah needed for this massive task. But tools he must have had! As we build and mould our family relationships, we may not have the sort of tools that we can see and hold, but our culture, values, attitudes and experiences shape our lives and those of the people we love, as surely as any plane, saw or hammer.

'I don't want to hear any more of your moaning, so have your bottle and shut up!' Marcy thumped the battered rag doll into the corner of the Wendy house, and tottered off to 'do the shopping' on a pair of perilously high-heeled black suede shoes from the dressing-up box. Play group was in full swing!

Even in these days of 'equal opportunities' and 'working women', most little girls, like Marcy, enjoy playing 'mummies' at some time in their lives. If they can persuade their brothers or their friends at play group to take part, then 'mummies and daddies' is even more fun! Watching and listening to them playing this game is a real eye-opener to any parent who happens to be nearby. If you, as a real-life

Mummy or Daddy, tend to shout and smack when angry, then the dolls are likely to have a hard time!

As children we adopt the attitudes and values of our parents without realizing it. When we in turn become parents, it is quite likely that we will unthinkingly reproduce those attitudes and values unless something makes us stop and ask: 'Is this what I really want to do? Is this the kind of life I really want to lead? Is this the kind of person I really want to be?'

_____ Where am I coming from? _____

As we try to work out what makes us tick as parents, we have to take into consideration at least two, and possibly three, different factors which will influence what we say and do whether we realize it or not:

- the ideas and attitudes absorbed from the culture of my nurturing family
- the ideas and attitudes that were around when I was a child, and are currently in vogue in the general culture from which I come
- the ideas and attitudes held by my church or 'faith' family.

■ What is culture?

Culture is a familiar word but one we may find difficult to explain. It has been described as 'a style of life, reflecting the shared viewpoint of a group of people'.

Our culture shapes our beliefs: about God, politics, the meaning of life.

It shapes our values: what we consider good, beautiful, or normal.

It shapes our customs: what we eat and how we eat it, how we dress, talk, relate to others, work, pray, and so on.

Culture varies from country to country. In many parts of the Third World, a woman who can't have a baby is despised and rejected by her family and friends. One tribe in Kenya even has a special word for a woman who dies childless – it means 'useless'. Such a woman would be buried outside the village, unwanted and unloved. In this instance we can see how a belief shapes a value, which in turn shapes behaviour and forms a culture. It isn't difficult to imagine the amazement of these African women if they heard that women in the West deliberately decide to refrain from having children, for career or other reasons.

As well as changing from country to country, culture also varies within countries. In these days of job mobility and economic migration, people from a variety of backgrounds and nationalities may live together in a relatively small area. In Britain a number of different cultures either blend or exist side by side. Indian, Pakistani, West Indian, Polish, Italian and Chinese people can all have homes in a medium-sized town like the one in which I live, and keep to their own ways of cooking, dressing, speaking and worshipping. Just to make things even more complicated, we still haven't managed to eradicate the so-called 'class' system in this country. Whether you feel that you belong to the 'working' class, the 'middle' class or the 'upper' class (or you are actively trying to ignore the whole thing!), this will also have an effect on your ideas about how life should be lived.

■ Just like his dad?

As we have already seen, the first people to influence us as children are our parents. We unconsciously receive 'scripts' from them about their beliefs and expectations of family life. These affect us very deeply. One teenager wrote to a magazine: 'My Dad says that the eldest girl in his family never gets married, and it's true that his aunty and eldest sister never did. I'm the eldest, and although I'm seventeen,

I've never had a boyfriend. I'm scared that it will come true for me too.'

John was brought up in an area of northern England where most of the men were involved in heavy industry and the shipyards. Sons tended to follow their fathers into similar jobs straight from school. In his city, relatives do still live within a few streets of one another, and his sister broke her engagement when her fiancé got a sales representative's job which would have meant a new home 100 miles from her family.

John decided that he didn't want to look for an engineering apprenticeship. When teachers encouraged him to stay on at school and then apply for college, his parents were puzzled and rather unenthusiastic, but they didn't interfere. When he decided to train as a social worker, however, and stay in the south-coast town where he had become actively involved in a church, this caused a real gulf between John and his parents. 'You'd think that I'm living on the moon,' he said ruefully, 'and the idea that I could actually enjoy spending a large part of Sunday at church or doing things with the youth group that I lead, just as Dad enjoys fishing and meeting up with his mates, makes no sense to them at all.'

■ On the street where you live

In addition to parental influence, we absorb beliefs and values from those we live and work with – which may or may not be the same as those held within our family circle. Stop and think for a moment. When you were growing up, what were the ideas of your neighbours and the friends with whom you played and went to school, and what were the ideas of the people you eventually worked with, about:

- swearing
- attitudes to people within the wider family

- the way those outside the family should be treated
- stealing and lying
- the value of human life
- the importance of material possessions
- the value of education
- God and going to church?

Did you feel at home within the culture in which you were living, or were your parents' attitudes so different that you felt uncomfortable and pulled in two directions? And what about your value system today? Is it simply a maturing of what you have grown up with, or something very different?

■ What about the faith factor?

One of the biggest areas of cultural change is the one that has taken place within the church. When Nancy and Tom were growing up (which wasn't that long ago) there were very definite values and patterns of behaviour expected in the Christian circles to which their parents belonged. Church attendance twice on Sunday was the norm, and in between services there were tidy walks in tidy clothes. There were restrictions in the forms of entertainment that were appropriate, and norms for behaviour which appear quaint today.

The problem was that like the Pharisees before them, church leaders had expanded the broad principles in the Bible into very detailed rules and regulations in a sincere but misguided attempt to promote godly living. And because there was still a respect for authority in the general culture of the day, this was reflected in the church. People may have muttered in secret, but it took a very determined individual to step far out of line.

As they prepared for marriage, Tom and Nancy both had to grapple with these things as a couple in the light of their own understanding of what the Bible had to say about faith and conduct. It was quite painful at times; they felt slightly disloyal questioning things that their parents had held to dearly – and since their views often differed from one another, their discussions were vigorous, to say the least! But even so, their basic approach to bringing up their children in the area of faith didn't stray far from the teaching that had been such an integral part of their own early lives.

Family, friends and faith are all important factors in our lives, and not one of us will bring exactly the same luggage from the past with us into the present. Even brothers and sisters often have a different view of their early life. Sometimes an onlooker might wonder whether they ever actually lived in the same home and had the same parents, so varied is their version of events.

With so many intertwining strands, understanding these things can be difficult. The chart on the next page can help you to see what elements from the past you want to take with you into your own family, and which need to be readjusted, or laid gently aside.

AREA	Family (my parents' values)	Friends (my culture's values)	Faith (my church's values)		My values (where have they come from?)
Marriage and family				⇑	
Faith and spiritual life				⇑	
Achievement & success at school, work, etc.				⇑	
Discipline and behaviour				⇑	
Relationships with those outside the nuclear family				⇑	
Time, pressures and priorities				⇑	

3

Interpreting the Chart

'God said to Noah, "You are to bring into the ark two of all living creatures, male and female, to keep them alive with you." ... Noah did everything just as God commanded him.'

Where am I going?

It had been one of those visits to the supermarket! Two-year-old Gavin had dropped a bottle of wine on to the eggs in his mother's trolley, almost dismantled an entire shelf of biscuits, taken a bite out of two very expensive peaches and forgotten to ask for the toilet in time. When we met in the queue for the checkout, he was having a tantrum because his mother wouldn't buy him the computer magazine whose brightly coloured cover had caught his eye.

'If he carries on like this, he will definitely be an only child, and probably an orphan into the bargain,' muttered Mary, as she struggled to unload her trolley with one hand, while restraining her screaming son with the other. 'Why didn't someone tell me what bringing up children is really like? Nothing I do seems to work. I feel as if I'm walking through a minefield without a mine detector. Whatever route I take, something is bound to blow up in my face.'

Bringing up a family has never been easy, but parenting in the 1990s seems to be more fraught with difficulty than ever, in spite of all the labour-saving devices that are available to lessen the physical load. Theories on how to guide children into adulthood abound, but as fast as they become fashionable, some 'expert' or other discredits them. So we are left with the unsettled feeling that the old 'charts' are out-dated and the new ones are untested and unreliable.

It's not just parents who are concerned. As the rate of family breakdown and juvenile crime increases, even government ministers are talking about the need for people to return to high standards and moral values – without, of course, defining what they are or suggesting how it might be done! Help is certainly needed, but where is it to come from? In years gone by, grannies and aunties were often on hand and up front with encouragement and advice. But nowadays they are likely to be living miles away, or busy 'doing their own thing' at work or in the community.

One source of help that previous generations have had, and which is still available today, is the Bible. With bookshops full of books by doctors, counsellors and psychologists, it may seem strange to consult this ancient book. But not only does the Bible contain the history and wisdom of the Jewish people (and Jews have always valued family life), it contains God's guidelines for living. The Ten Commandments and the teaching of Jesus are all there to give us broad principles for how we should relate to one another.

As we look at the Bible we can see that much of the actual outworking of day-to-day family life is both rooted in and influenced by the culture of the time. It is clearly both impossible and undesirable to try to transfer those patterns over nearly 2,000 years and hundreds of miles!

But what we can do is to look at the guidelines by which the nation of Israel was intended to live in the Bible, as a working demonstration of how God wanted relationships with himself and other people to be. Then, if we accept that although history and cultures change, God remains the same, we have principles for family living that we can use as a plumbline against which to measure our understanding and performance.

God's intention for families

God is in favour of relationships, and he works through them. God designed human beings to relate together in families, and he created us with distinct dimensions to our lives. We may grow in some areas more fully than others, but each one of us has

- a spiritual potential
- a mental or intellectual potential
- a social and emotional potential
- a physical potential.

Each of these are potentials that we can develop and enjoy. God chose to place us in family units so that we can help each other to learn and change as we share life together. We all belong to a nurturing or human family which we join initially by birth (and may add to by adoption or marriage) and we all experience its benefits, joys and sorrows to a greater or lesser degree.

So families are intended to be good news. They were designed by God to be a loving and secure environment where each person can be helped and encouraged to develop fully, and where children and adults alike are valued and cherished for themselves, just as they are. When families operate as God intended, they form the bedrock upon which the whole structure of a stable society is built.

As we look at the Bible we can see how important families are. These are some of the things that the Bible teaches about the place of families in the overall scheme of things.

■ Families have a social dimension

Today we are beginning to see what happens in a society when family life breaks down. Much of the Old Testament law focused on how relationships between people should be conducted, and there were specific laws to protect the well-being of the family.

■ Families have an economic dimension

The ability of each family unit to provide for itself is portrayed as the ideal, but God has a lot to say throughout the Bible about our responsibilities towards those in our families who are in need, particularly elderly relatives and widows. How much this can or should continue to be taken over by the Welfare State is an issue that is being increasingly debated in an ageing population.

■ Families have a spiritual dimension

Many of us subconsciously share the belief that talking about religious beliefs (if it happens at all!) is the prerogative of grown ups, and that any teaching that children receive is best handled by specialists within the church services or Sunday children's groups. But the Bible is emphatic that parents have a very definite responsibility to teach their children about this dimension of life. As Moses gave the commandments of God to the Israelites he said, 'Impress them on your children. Talk about them at home... when you walk along the road... when you lie down... when you get up.'

But this spiritual dimension goes beyond learning commandments. God, too, is a person, and as we see and enjoy good relationships within families it helps us, and the world around us, to understand a relational God.

So families are important. But what does the Bible say about God's plan for our individual families, and the foundations that we need to lay as parents?

_____ Wanted – the perfect parent! _____

If you embarked on parenthood with every intention of being the 'perfect' parent of a 'model' child, join the club! Once the baby arrives, we rapidly discover that we are not only imperfect, but that we also have the potential for being an absolute disaster. Help is urgently needed. It is a huge relief to know that God's unconditional love and forgiveness covers our mistakes as parents, as well as all our other shortcomings.

From the moment of birth, every human being embarks on a process of separation and growth which continues into early adult life and beyond. As our physical, emotional, mental and spiritual needs are met we move towards wholeness and maturity. But just as in a greenhouse certain conditions need to be present if the delicate seedlings are to grow, so as parents we will see our family relationships blossom most freely if we ourselves have a deep and growing relationship with God. God can then work in our lives so that the qualities that reflect his parenthood of us are gradually produced. As a heavenly parent, God offers us:

* unconditional love and acceptance
* absolute and ungrudging forgiveness
* untiring commitment
* protection and provision for our needs
* consistent discipline
* absolute freedom within clearly defined limits.

This is what our children also need. The importance of the first five foundational areas is easy to recognize although often hard to put into practice, but the boundaries for behaviour are often hotly debated. However, if we are looking for guidance, the Bible does have some specific things to say.

God's guidelines for living

The Ten Commandments have formed a basis for law as well as personal conduct down the centuries. The first four commandments refer to our attitude towards God, the next three to our relationship with other people, and the last three give guidance about how we should view property. So we have the following:

1. No other gods – not God and something else...
2. God is a spiritual being – we must not try to 'earth' him with objects that could easily become idols.
3. God's name is holy – no swearing or taking it lightly.
4. Keeping one day set apart for God is a symbol of his importance in our lives.

5. Honour parents – give attention to their commands, take care of them in their need.
6. Respect the sacredness of human life.
7. Respect the fundamental importance of marriage.

8. Respect the property of others.
9. Respect the immense value of another's good name.
10. No coveting – covetousness is a form of idolatry and is the root cause of sin against people and property.

The fifth and seventh commandments are keys to the stability of the family as a whole.

In the Gospels and the writings of the first Christians there is no clear description of what a family should be or how it should be structured, but there are specific

22

instructions about relationships within families. These deal particularly with the attitudes of husbands and wives to one another, the way that parents should handle their children and how children should respond. So what do they say?

1. Husbands and wives are to love and respect one another – a strong marriage helps children to feel secure.
2. Parents have the responsibility to love, protect, provide for and discipline their children, and to teach them about spiritual matters.
3. Children are to obey and honour their parents.

Does it surprise you that the instructions for earthly parents and children are reflected almost exactly in the way that God deals with his children and what he asks of us in return? Looking at the Bible as a whole, we can say that if we want to have family relationships that reach their full potential, then we must each work at

- loving and honouring God
- loving and honouring ourselves, because we are precious and valuable to God
- loving and honouring others as much as we love ourselves.

Perhaps you find that disappointing. Maybe you were hoping for some profound new insight that would solve all your problems. This sounds almost too simple – almost simplistic – and has been said so often before. Well, parenting God's way is like so many other facets of Christian truth: it may have been preached, but has it been practised?

4
Choosing My Course

'The waters rose and increased greatly on the earth, and the ark floated on the surface of the water.'

When we have a clearer idea of what factors from the past have shaped us, and when we have established some firm guidelines for family life, we will be in a better position to decide what we want to change, and what we want to hold on to and develop. In an ideal world, we would have this self-knowledge before we embarked on parenthood. Unfortunately life is rarely that tidy, and we generally set out in carefree ignorance. It is only when we hit a patch of choppy water on our 'Voyage of Discovery' that we begin to ask ourselves some searching questions. 'Is this the size and shape of "Ark" that we really need,' we may ask, 'and where are we sailing to anyway?'

If this is your situation at the moment, don't despair. If I can change the travelling metaphor from the ancient world to the 1990s, an intercontinental aircraft has a series of flaps on its wings. When the pilot wishes to alter his course he makes very small adjustments to the angle of these flaps. In this way the plane is steered in a new direction with a minimum of stress on the passengers or the structure of the plane. We too will find that even small adjustments in attitudes and actions can have a considerable effect on the direction in which we are moving. But first of all, of course, it helps to know where we want to go.

A motorist was looking for a hotel in a very remote part of the country, and became thoroughly lost in a tangle of narrow lanes where there seemed to be neither signposts nor people. At last, to his relief, he came across an elderly farmer leaning on a gate gazing reflectively at his cows. The motorist stopped and asked whether the old man could direct him. After a long silence, the farmer replied, 'Well, I knows the place, but if I was you I wouldn't set out for there from here!'

As parents we might wish that we did not have to set out on our journey 'from here', if the place we are in at the moment is difficult or unhappy. But like that unfortunate motorist, we can't do anything other than start from where we are. We need to take a good look at the present as it is, decide where we want to get to, and then see if we can find a route between the two that we can cope with.

Home sweet home?

It was the beginning of the school holidays, and a number of special events all seemed to be on in a very short space of time – from the regional agricultural show, to the latest children's film at the cinema. I checked the kitchen calendar and, without telling my children, planned a week of hectic activity. Unexpectedly, two of their friends came to stay, and joined us on all our outings with great enthusiasm. When I took our visitors to the station for their homeward journey, my nine-year-old looked at me and grinned. 'We have had a nice week,' he said. 'Did you do it because you wanted to, or because you wanted to make a good impression?'

I laughed. I wasn't guilty on that occasion, but I knew what he meant. All too often the saying that 'home is the place that we are loved the best, and behave the worst!'

rings uncomfortably true. And even if 'home' doesn't live up to our expectations in terms of the love we receive, it still tends to be the place where we expect people to put up with us however we behave.

We all need a 'safe place' where we can get away from the pressures and anxieties of the world around us. But the four walls which surround the place in which we live don't create the safe place; they just form the outer shell. The key factor that decides whether the home is a happy place where we feel secure, or full of bitterness and unease, is the attitude of the people who live there.

The Bible has a lot to say about the way that we should treat one another. The early Christian leader St Paul wrote to one church: 'Don't worship the good things of life... throw away all these rotten garments of anger, hatred, cursing and dirty language. Don't tell lies to one another.' And to another church he pleaded: 'Practise tender- hearted mercy and kindness to others. Be gentle and ready to forgive; never hold grudges. Remember the Lord forgave you, so you must forgive others. Most of all let love guide your life... let the peace of heart which comes from Christ always be present in your lives... And always be thankful.'

Which of these or other similar attitudes are shaping the prevailing atmosphere in your home? We often say that 'an Englishman's home is his castle' – meaning that we consider it to be a place from which we can shut out anything we think of as the enemy. Unfortunately, we are all such fallible people that, instead of building a fortress that keeps the enemy out, we allow our own negative attitudes to sneak in like Trojan horses and set up camp. So instead of a safe place, our home becomes a trap, and our family life the biggest battlefield of all. So we're angry with our boss, but choose instead to bring our anger home and take it out on the children; our child's broken friendship at school becomes an excuse for sulkiness at home.

Fortress or walled garden?

Imagine that you had to go and live in the desert, and you had the choice of two 'desirable residences' (as the estate agent would describe them). One home is a fortress with watch towers situated at intervals along the massive walls. Inside are broken buildings, small windows, barred doors and sweltering heat. Those who live there are barely relaxed. They have to be prepared for attack at any time – as much from those living with them as from those creeping up on them outside the walls.

The second home is also sheltered by a high wall. It's a simple building set in a beautiful garden. A fountain sends water soaring through the air to splash gently into the sunlit pool below. There are sweetly scented plants, and thickly leaved trees give patches of deep shade. The sun is just as hot, as it blazes down on this home, but here people rest and recover from the wounds that they have received out in the desert, before going out to do battle again.

Do either of these two imaginary homes sound like the place where you live now, or describe your family situation?

Of course we can't really choose between a walled garden or a mini-fortress in which to set up house. But we can decide whether we'll accept a situation where the atmosphere is tense and people are constantly waging a war of words – criticizing, arguing and trying to do one another down. Or whether instead we will consciously work towards having the kind of home where you can sense a different atmosphere as you walk through the door. Here people are loved, encouraged, helped and served. It isn't perfect by any means, but when things go wrong efforts are made to put them right, rather than burying them under the carpet!

God wants to share our home and family life with us. If we ask him to, he can help us to identify the reasons for conflict within, and gradually transform the most tumbledown ruin into a place that brings pleasure to all who live there, as well as those who visit it.

What kind of
_____ family do I want to be part of? _____

Many firms and voluntary bodies have written vision statements which are intended to sum up what the organization is in business for. Few parents are likely to have thought about their families in quite such formal terms but many of us may have said things like:

'I want to give my children all the opportunities that I missed out on.'

'When my dad wasn't at work he was out fishing (or playing golf / at church meetings / down at the pub). I want my kids to have a father.'

'Money was tight when I was a child. I want my family to be financially secure.'

'The best times we had were on holiday with the whole family – grandparents, aunts, the lot. I'd like to recreate that sense of togetherness for my children.'

Interestingly, we tend to notice first what we see as lacking in our childhood, rather than the more positive things, although both are important. Knowing what we *don't* want is sometimes easier to define than what we *do*, but here are two lists of hopes and fears for family life suggested by a group of parents who met to discuss parenting. They had children ranging in age from a few months to twenty-six years.

Can you identify with any of these hopes and fears? You might well want to add others. What would you say was most important to you?

HOPES

My hopes for my family

To enjoy good, open relationships
To be hardworking
To have time to be together
To be able to provide for each
    other
To worship and pray together
To have an attitude of
    thankfulness
To be generous and forgiving
To have concern for others
To be trustworthy and honest
To be hospitable and caring
To be confident and successful
To have a good self-image

Our hopes as parents

Aim to let children be themselves
Stay friends with them as adults
Maintain our marriage
    relationship without children
Receive from our children
    graciously
Aim to let them hear God's call on
    their lives

We hope our children will...

Find a suitable marriage partner
Have a fulfilling career
Be obedient to God
Develop their individuality
Maintain close family ties

FEARS

My fears for my family

Relationships breaking
    down as we get older
Too much busyness
Redundancy – lack of
    resources
Loss of religious faith as we
    mature
Not sharing same values
Being criticized by others
Children have unhelpful
    friends
Serious illness / death
Trouble with authority
Selfish and materialistic
Failing to love enough
Poor self-image / failure

Our fears as parents

Make mistakes and cause
    permanent damage to
    personalities
Be too strict / not strict
    enough
Emptiness when they leave
    home

What is my 'parenting style'?

My eldest son enjoys reading books on management, rejoicing in such titles as *Leaders and Followers*, *Manage by Encouragement*, *Finding Your Management Style*, and a host of others. Leaders of industry and professional organizations recognize that there are some ways of dealing with people and getting the results that you want, which are more successful than others. They are quick to pass those techniques on to their managers.

As parents too, we will adopt a certain style of handling our children, often either unthinkingly copied from our parents, or vigorously opposed to the parenting that we experienced. Sometimes what we do naturally isn't the most helpful way to do the job, and so we need to ask ourselves:

■ Am I a 'do-it-my-way parent'?

Am I locked in to a very rigid framework of behaviour and beliefs which I insist that my children stick to, even if I'm not very consistent about following them myself? Is 'Never mind what I do – do as I say' the actual if unspoken principle that I follow? Do I expect to do everything for my children, even when they are quite capable of doing things for themselves, because I'm afraid that they'll make mistakes that would be harmful to themselves or others?

Have I been brought up to believe that this is what a 'good parent' does, and at least things get done properly this way?

If I find myself trying to control my children by these means, perhaps I need to ask myself: 'What am I afraid of? Why is perfection so important to me? And why do I have so little trust in God's ability to lead my children to choose the good without being forced into it?'

■ Am I a 'do-as-you-like parent'?

Do I usually take the easy way out? Under the guise of being a freedom-loving and progressive parent, do I give in to my children, but constantly worry about the outcome of their actions? Having done this, do I then project my fears on to them by nagging about the possible results of what I have allowed them to do?

This kind of parenting, far from being ultra-loving, is often rooted in fear of rejection if the children resist being disciplined, or an unrecognized but deep-seated resentment of children who take up so much time and energy.

■ Am I a 'responsible-but-releasing parent'?

Have I thought through what I believe in and what I am trying to achieve as a parent, while realizing that there is always more to learn, and that there are areas in which I've still got plenty of growing to do? Do I see our home essentially as a harbour where our children are equipped for the voyage of life? Is my aim to train and support them, encouraging them to make little coastal sorties, until eventually they have enough skills to set sail out of the harbour and face the open seas alone?

What is the effect of these parenting styles?

A 'do-it-my-way' style of parenting may look as if it brings very good results initially. Children brought up in this way may seem to be very well behaved, but the good behaviour is often only surface deep because they have never been encouraged to think through issues for themselves. Although they may appear to be outwardly responsible and well disciplined, there is little deep-seated responsibility or self-discipline. This is largely because the children have been ruled by fear of parental disapproval, rather than taking on these attitudes from choice. The result tends to be that they either become fearful adults, dependent on others for their sense of values, or they toss all restraint to the wind as soon as they are able to do so.

If the 'big stick' approach has this effect, it can be very tempting to assume that the 'do-as-you-like' option may be the better way. It was certainly tried in the Sixties, and the results were very mixed! As we have already seen, children (and people) do need freedom, but it is freedom within clearly defined limits. Children who aren't given any boundaries for their behaviour, or who have ever-changing boundaries which are very inconsistently enforced, are often very insecure. Not only that, but they may well become inwardly angry and then feel guilty about having such negative reactions towards parents whom they want to love and respect.

I was having one of our routine 'What time do I have to be in? – No one has to be in that early!' arguments with my teenage daughter, when insight got the better of indignation and she said, 'Sarah's mum says she doesn't care what time Sarah gets in. But I'm not sure that it's really the time she's talking about. I think she means she doesn't care full stop. And that's what Sarah feels, come to think about it!'

Of course, we aren't consistent and self-disciplined all the time, but children whose parents do feel confident about what they are doing and are generally consistent – yet flexible enough to listen and change their views when there is good reason to do so – tend to launch responsible and confident offspring into the world. Parenting is a process of letting go from infancy to adulthood, and at every stage of growth there will be fresh opportunities to encourage our children to make their own decisions, and increase their areas of responsibilities.

Until they reach the stage of taking total responsibility for their lives, if we judge that what our children are up to doesn't offend society's laws or God's laws, or harm themselves or others, we may like to ask, as my friend Jenny does, 'Will it matter when he or she is twenty-one?' Sometimes, of course, the answer is yes, and then a course of action may have to be insisted upon. But it's amazing how much steam can be taken out of the simmering cauldron of family tensions by judicious application of that little safety valve!

_____ Do I need to make changes? _____

The humorist who said 'a woman's place is in the wrong' might well have said the same about parents! Much as we may want to be ideal parents for the children we love so much, any look at definitions is almost guaranteed to make us feel like handing in our resignation. We identify failures so much more easily than we can define our successes. But the good news is that, although we will never be 'model' parents or 'perfect' parents (only God is a perfect parent, and look at the kind of children that he has!) we can be good-enough parents for our particular children.

What kind of parents
_____ do my children need? _____

'Just wait till your father gets home. Then there'll be trouble.'

'Sorry! I don't know anything about the children's timetable. I leave all that sort of thing to the wife!'

Father-dominated, mother in charge, or we're-in-this-together – what kind of job-sharing on the parenting front goes on in your house, and how would you define the roles of a mother and a father anyway? Traditionally, the man has been seen as the one who provides and protects, and the woman's job has been to nurture and care, but these are not rigid boundaries which cannot be crossed. Whether through economic necessity or the desire to use their hard-won education, many women are choosing to work outside the home. By the end of the century the percentage of women in work (out of the total who could work) will be as high for women as for men. Conversely, unemployment for men may bring some a greater role in nurturing and caring for their children.

Although we generally refer to God as Father as Jesus did (and perhaps tend to picture him as primarily a provider and protector), the Bible actually draws a picture of someone who holds within one personality all those qualities that we tend to label 'male' and 'female'. The Psalmist wrote: 'As a father has compassion on his children, so the Lord has compassion on those who fear him.' But one of the Old Testament prophets said: 'Can a mother forget the baby at her breast and have no compassion on the child she has borne? Though she may forget, God will not forget you.'

As John White writes in *Parents in Pain*, 'God... is not father in the sense of not being mother. He can accurately be referred to as father-mother God. He is the source of all that is motherly and fatherly, and we are all, both fathers and mothers, called to be like him.'

So both parents are important, and both have a unique contribution to offer, depending on their personalities and gifts, as well as their sex. Of course if, for whatever reason, single parenthood is forced upon us, it is possible to compensate for the input of the absent parent to a certain extent by welcoming the support, encouragement and example of a 'significant other' such as a grandparent, teacher, youth leader or family friend. Many lone parents, with or without these resources, do an excellent job in bringing up their children. The committed love and nurture of one parent will be better than the neglect of two. But single parents often have an extra rough road to travel, and, where both parents are available, it is God's ideal for them both to be actively involved in their children's lives.

What kind of parents do children need? In addition to love, acceptance, commitment to provide and protect, and consistent discipline, I would suggest that children need parents who know where they want to go, and are prepared to give reasons for their choice of route – while listening to requests to explore another way of getting to the destination. And in order for all this to happen, we need to be acutely aware of the vital importance of time invested in our families. For all children need parents who will give them time: time to listen, time to laugh and time to learn together.

Boswell, the biographer of Samuel Johnson, often spoke of a day when his father had taken him fishing, and of all the special memories and lessons for living that that day had given him. Curious to know what Boswell's father had felt about the expedition, a journalist of the time checked to see what the father had written about that day. There were just nine words:

'Gone fishing today with my son – a day wasted.'

5
Maintaining the Engine

'The waters flooded the earth for a hundred and fifty days.'

If we were tuning an engine, we would need to be a mechanic. And if we are to be 'good' parents, we need... well what? What *are* the skills needed? For me, it has revolved around three key skills: being able to communicate, knowing how to listen, and disciplining with a balance between freedom and firm boundaries.

KEY SKILL 1
Communication – sending the right signals

The little boy next door was dressed in his best, ready for a friend's birthday party. He was whiling away the waiting time by playing with a pile of builder's sand. Suddenly there was an anguished shriek from his mother, as she discovered what he was up to.

'Look at your trousers, Jonathon!' she scolded. 'And we might as well throw away those socks. You know you're not allowed to play with that sand!' 'But I played with it yesterday,' objected Jonathon. 'You didn't tell me I couldn't play with it now.' 'You had your old jeans on then.' His mother sent him on his way to change with an exasperated smack. 'You are getting rebellious.'

36

From the position of an uninvolved observer, I felt sorry for them both. Such a simple thing: Sue had failed to tell Jonathon that the rules from yesterday no longer applied today. Yet that small breakdown in communication resulted in a miserable beginning to what should have been a very happy afternoon. But communication is like that. It is a word that many of us use often, understand little, and put into practice badly. In fact, counsellors tell us that 80% of relationship problems stem from a basic lack of communication skills.

So what does the word 'communication' mean in the first place? The dictionary defines it as the 'imparting of news, information or feelings', which sounds simple enough. But communication is a subtle thing. It takes place on five different levels:

- level 5: cliché – everything is 'fine'
- level 4: reporting facts about others
- level 3: sharing my ideas and judgements
- level 2: sharing my feelings and emotions
- level 1: complete personal openness.

Imagine the scene. Margaret has met Pam on the bus, and from your seat behind them you hear the following conversation:

Pam:	Margaret! Haven't seen you for ages. How are you?
Margaret:	*(tonelessly)* Fine.
Pam:	Where's Johnny?
Margaret:	He started school last week.
Pam:	Where's he gone?
Margaret:	Parkfield Lower. We had a choice of two. I hope we've chosen right – you hear so many different opinions.

Pam:	You must be looking forward to having some time to yourself now after... how long... fifteen years with pre-schoolers?
Margaret:	Not really. It brings a lump to my throat just to look at his school bag lying in the hall.
Pam:	You'll miss him at first, of course!
Margaret:	Miss him? My whole life seems to have come to an end. I feel utterly useless and completely lost – the days seem endless.

It is, of course, unlikely that Margaret would have moved right through the stages of communication in a public place unless Pam was a particularly close friend and Margaret was feeling very desperate – most of us would stop at 5 or 4 and certainly by level 3. But this example shows how real communication might take place, because it occurs when I 'openly and honestly share my thoughts, longings, dreams, fears and needs with you. At the same time I do my best to understand your feelings, so that I can meet your needs.' It is a rare and precious thing when it happens.

If communication is such a key skill in keeping the machinery of family relationships running smoothly, it is obviously a good idea to improve our performance as much as we can. Perhaps the first thing we need to understand is how we get our messages across.

Turn your 'radio' on

There must be very few homes without at least one radio, bringing us information or entertainment at the press of a button. Messages sent from some distant radio station travel across the airwaves to be picked up by the radio so that we can hear them. Exactly the same process occurs when we talk to one another face to face, but in this situation, the person talking or doing something is the radio station, the person listening or watching is the radio receiver, and the message may be sent out in actions as well as words, because an amazing 70% of communication actually occurs without a word being spoken.

_____ Getting the message across _____

Stuart and Jenny hadn't been getting on too well, and went their separate ways one morning feeling really fed up with their relationship. During the day, they both decided to try to put things right. Jenny planned a special evening meal, despatched the children to their grandparents for the night, and did all she could to create a relaxed atmosphere for an evening of talking their problems through. When Stuart arrived home, he bounded into the house with a large package from the DIY shop under his arm. Oblivious of the soft lights and succulent smells, he changed into old clothes ready to put up some long-awaited shelves in the bathroom – as soon as Jenny came out of the shower. They were both trying to say 'I'm sorry and I love you' but were using different languages.

We all have a way of communicating with which we feel the most at home. Jenny, like many women, conveys her message through words first of all, although setting an atmosphere that feels right is also important to her. Stuart often retreats into silence when things upset him, but finds the most natural way to express himself is through actions. He prefers to keep the talking short and to the point. When couples or families don't understand the way others within the circle communicate, there can be a lot of misunderstandings.

_____ Reading the signs _____

Since so much communication goes on without a word being spoken, learning to read body language is a very useful accomplishment. Try turning the sound right down on the television during a programme with plenty of action in it, and see how much of the plot you can understand. Sit in a cafe or on the bus and watch the unspoken communication that goes on. Stand by the school gates and watch small children coming out to meet the adults who are waiting for them. Do the words and actions always match?

'Say what you mean'

'What you say is what you are. Ha ha!' Does that chant still ring round playgrounds today? Children use words differently from adults. For them words don't have the subtle shades of meaning that adults give them. They expect that what we say, we mean. So a remark like 'Would you like to put your toys away now, so that we can go to the shops?' will probably be taken as a question that can have a 'yes' or 'no' answer, when what we probably mean is that it is time to go shopping, and there is no choice about it.

What we say and the way we act while saying it, can also give confused messages. My father-in-law died very suddenly during the night, and I took the children to school the next day without telling them anything other than that Daddy had had to go to Granny's because Grandpa had been taken to hospital. It was my birthday, and when my husband returned home we decided between us that having told the children (then aged six, eight and ten) we would carry on with the special birthday meal we had organized 'so that they won't be disappointed'. The children took the news of their grandfather's death fairly philosophically, and we carried on with the evening as planned.

At bedtime my eight-year-old gave me a very puzzled look. 'Are you sad about Grandpa dying?' he asked.

'Yes, of course I am,' I answered, thinking what a tear-filled birthday it had been. He shook his head in disbelief. 'Well, you don't seem sad,' he said.

Of course, it doesn't have to be such a major event as a bereavement to cause us to say one thing while feeling and

40

acting another. 'No, of course I'm not in a bad mood!' spoken through gritted teeth as you slam the door really says, 'I'm very angry, but I'm denying it because it isn't OK to feel that way'.

What do we
_____ need to communicate? _____

The need to know that we are important to someone, and that we are valued and valuable just because we are us, is something that is absolutely basic to every human being. As parents, helping our children to feel good about themselves – to know that they are unique, special, made just as they are for a particular purpose and unreservedly loved both by the God who created them and the parents who have the privilege of bringing them up – is the most important thing we can do.

Self-esteem is the value people put upon themselves. High self-esteem is the ability to feel good about being who you are. Many parents have problems with helping their children in this area because they themselves have low self-esteem and a poor self-image. Christian parents who are, perhaps, particularly aware of their inbuilt tendency to live their own way, rather than God's, may feel that it is impossible to feel good about themselves. But although the Christian faith makes people more sensitive to their shortcomings, it also offers the solution. Thankfully, with God's help, there's always the opportunity to come to God for forgiveness and to receive from him both the strength to change what needs to be changed and the ability to accept what can't be changed – and hopefully, too, the wisdom to tell the difference!

When we are comfortable with being the people that we are (while recognizing that life is a constant process of growth and change) we can give our children positive messages about:

■ Being who they are

When we see them as God sees them – a gift from him, and someone to care for on his behalf, rather than an accident, a prop for an ailing relationship, or a plaything for us to enjoy – we can genuinely help them to feel that they have been born for a purpose and are accepted and lovable just as they are.

We let them know this by telling them that we love them, that they are special and fun to be with in a way that they understand and are comfortable with, rather than in the language that we use most easily. One of my sons is not a great talker, and he relates much more easily to an action that demonstrates love, or a note that expresses it, rather than a long speech about it. Touch is important, too. When she was tiny, our younger daughter loved to have her feet tickled. An action which to me was almost unbearable sent her into raptures! Hugging and kissing, hands available to hold, a cuddle on the settee while reading or watching television, all demonstrate love – we just need to discover what communicates best to our particular children.

■ Making their unique contribution

Children need to know that we think they have something to offer to others; that they are capable of dealing with life's challenges and succeeding in the tasks they have to tackle. All too often we give negative messages – 'Don't touch that; it's too sharp; you'll cut yourself.' The idea, once suggested, is likely to bring about the outcome that we fear. If we say, 'You are holding that carefully; make sure you cut down on to the board', then an accident will probably be avoided.

■ Handling their own thoughts and feelings

Children do think about how the world works – you've only got to be with a pre-schooler at the 'why' stage to know that – and they need to be encouraged to think things through for themselves. Here again the temptation can be to tell them how they should think, and give them easy answers, rather than allowing them to come to their own conclusions. They also have very strong feelings, and they need to know that it is all right to have feelings, and if necessary be helped to express them appropriately. Parents often feel very uncomfortable when their children express negative emotions, but it isn't the emotion that we feel, but what we do with it that is important.

■ Being true to themselves and their own convictions

We read and talk a great deal about 'peer pressure' today. Children are often great conformists, hating to be different. Perhaps this is because we, as parents, have a hard time standing out from the crowd as well. But just as we need to think for ourselves before we decide what to do or believe, we need to afford that privilege to our children. We will obviously want to share our values in words and actions, but whether or not our children choose to adopt them is ultimately their decision.

When they are young they tend to accept our ideas without question. But as their experience of life grows wider, they will learn that there are many points of view which have to be weighed and sifted, and we will need to give them the freedom to do that. Teenagers in particular will find it easier to take a stand about things that they don't want to go along with, if it is genuinely their decision, rather than one which has been imposed from outside.

What do we want to avoid _____ in our communication? _____

As parents we have a great deal of power over our children's lives, because what we say to them or about them when young tends to be accepted by them without question. If we say it often enough it becomes part of their belief system about themselves, and shapes their behaviour. This is why the 'labels' that we had put on us as children are often very difficult to shift when we are adults. Perhaps they are beliefs such as:

- I'm hopeless with money
- I can't sing in tune
- Good things never come easily to me
- My sister has the looks in our family.

We label children when we say negative things to them directly: 'You're always the one who starts the trouble!' We label children when we talk about them in a negative way to other people, in their hearing: 'Oh, Gemma wouldn't want to go to the party on her own – she's far too shy.'

Even positive labelling can be damaging because people may feel that they have to live up to being 'clever' or 'pretty' or 'witty', because if they don't they will be viewed as failures and won't be acceptable.

How can we avoid the 'label trap'?

Recognize the labels that we use for different members of the family. With older children it can be fun to try to catch one another doing it, and award prizes for a label-free day! Make a conscious effort to avoid labelling. Like any habit, it takes time to change, so don't be too hard on yourself if it doesn't happen immediately. You could try to replace the label with positive messages that don't judge the behaviour but describe it accurately, and say how you feel about it. So rather than, 'You are a good girl to go shopping for Granny,' you might say 'Thank you for carrying Granny's shopping home. It was a real help to me.' Or instead of 'You are so careless with your belongings,' you could try, 'Please will you pick up that game. It bothers me to see things being spoiled.'

All that may seem very laborious and unnatural, but it is worth attempting when we think about the way that positive and negative communication from our own parents has shaped our lives. It is, after all, 'better to build children, than to repair adults'.

KEY SKILL 2
Listening – receiving you loud and clear!

'It is impossible to over-emphasize the immense need men have to be really listened to, to be taken seriously, to be understood... No one can develop freely in this world and find a full life, without feeling understood by at least one person.'

Paul Tournier

It's one thing to send out your messages, and another thing entirely to have them heard and understood. We've already thought about some of the problems of being the 'transmitter' and the important messages we might want to send out. But being the 'receiver' is the other half of the communication equation, and is every bit as important. There are lots of things that we need to communicate to one another, but they fall into two broad groups: facts and information, and emotions and feelings.

Of course, it's all too easy to get factual information wrong, because we don't express ourselves clearly, or don't listen properly. But the area in which we most need to sharpen up our listening skills is sorting out what is being expressed in terms of emotion and feelings.

Some people live their lives on a pretty even keel emotionally while others are much more 'up and down', but we all get upset from time to time. Sometimes it's just a fleeting thing, but at other times we feel so battered by this huge wave of feeling that we can't think straight. It's then that we have a pressing need to be listened to in such a way that we can unload the feelings, and then stand back from the emotion or problem and see what is really happening.

When we see our children upset, we very much want to 'make it all better' for them. Often, rather than really listening to what they are saying, we are busy trying to think how to advise them, how to shield them from the problem or pain, or how to get them to forget about it by distracting them into thinking about something else. If we succeed in doing any or all of these things, we may appear to have helped for the moment, but all that has really happened is that the emotion has been pushed down for the time being, and will undoubtedly shoot up to the surface again with even more force next time the problem arises.

Silent listening

An adult or a child who is very upset is often too full of emotion to be able to think through a problem clearly, but they don't want to hear our solution! One of the best ways that we can help them is to listen while they struggle to put their feelings into words, without commenting or criticizing. This means that we put our own needs to one side, and focus completely on the one who is speaking.

If we listen with a loving attitude, the speaker will sense that he is accepted and cared for. If we listen with our eyes as well as our ears, we will learn more, because the way he stands or sits, smiles or scowls, clenches his fists or twists his legs into knots will also tell us a great deal. If we refrain from interrupting, and speak only if we need to clarify some point that we don't understand, we shall probably find that we need to say very little, and yet the person speaking will feel comforted and understood.

Silent listening is hard, but it works

It can be very difficult to come to terms with the fact that our children are individuals in their own right with an inner life that is theirs alone. If they are expressing a point of view that we may not approve of, or find difficult to accept, it is hard to listen without trying to 'put them right'. It's also hard to resist the temptation to take over and try to solve the problem for them, rather than sitting with them while they work out their own solution, and only making suggestions if asked.

Giving someone else this degree of attention is hard work, and is best not done standing up or on an empty stomach! Sometimes we are too distracted by our own problems and pressures to listen properly, and we may need to say so and arrange a time when we can give our undivided attention. But this should probably be a last resort, as most of us aren't good at sharing how we feel, and if the moment is lost, it tends to be lost for ever.

Sometimes it's hard to listen silently, because we have poor listening habits. We can listen five times faster than we can speak, so there are quite a few gaps when our concentration can wander. During this time we may easily miss what is actually being said because we:

- are too busy thinking of what we want to say as soon as the other person pauses for breath
- ignore the things we don't want to hear, and focus only on the points that seem important to us
- feel irritated or bored by the person who is speaking and dismiss their problem as unimportant
- start thinking about our own problems!

We may think that we're giving the impression of being all attention, but the person who is speaking almost always

47

senses that we're not really listening, and will find it hard to continue with what they want to say.

Sometimes silent
_____ **listening is not enough** _____

'I can never tell you what you said, but only what I heard. I will have to rephrase what you said and check it out with you to make sure that what left your mind and heart, arrived in my mind and heart intact, and without distortion.'

John Powell

Listening quietly and with our full attention is always a very important ingredient of helping someone to unload emotional pressures or sort out a problem, but sometimes we need to take a more active role. This is where active or reflective listening skills come in.

Sometimes we need to repeat what we have heard in our own words, to make sure that what we think we have heard is actually what the speaker meant. This helps the other person to be clear about what they meant as well. We do this automatically when given instructions on how to find our way somewhere. We want to be sure that we've heard things accurately.

Sometimes we may find it helpful to reflect the emotion that appears to underlie what the child is saying, by choosing appropriate 'feeling' words. For instance, Mary comes home in tears having been pushed out of a friend's game and says: 'Paula is horrible and I don't want to play with her ever again.'

Our automatic reaction might be: 'Oh, you're always falling out; you'll soon make it up.' But a more helpful response might be: 'You sound really cross and upset with her.'

The first response shuts down the conversation and dismisses the emotion felt as unimportant. The second one acknowledges her pain, and allows her to work towards a solution. We can't know for certain how anyone is feeling, because different people respond to similar situations with a variety of emotions. But reflecting the emotions that seem to be coming across will make it possible for the speaker to correct us if necessary.

Open and closed questions

Sometimes children find it difficult to share what is going on within them. That is where 'open questions' can help the conversational ball to start rolling. An 'open' question is one that doesn't dictate or limit the answer required. A 'closed' question usually limits the child to a 'yes' or 'no' answer and tends to close the conversation down.

When my children were teenagers, I tried to be in the kitchen when they came home from school if I possibly could. A simple question like 'How was your day?' as they came in through the back door was usually answered with 'Fine', said in a variety of tones. A 'Fine' said cheerfully required little follow up, but when it was grunted or groaned out, tea and sympathy offered with an open question like: 'It doesn't sound as if it was too good – do you want to tell me about it?' was far more likely to gain a response than 'Are you feeling cross?'

As with all new skills, 'silent' and 'active' listening can seem very cumbersome and uncomfortable when we first try to use them, but they can soon become part of our natural way of communicating with one another, and might even result in us as partners and parents being really heard and understood.

KEY SKILL 3
Discipline – boundaries and freedom

'I really dread having Mary to stay. She's into everything, and her mother does nothing to stop her. No idea of how to discipline a child, that's Jane's problem.'

'Oh dear! I suppose she's one of those modern parents – believes the little darlings have to "express themselves".'

'We don't see Gary or Melissa in church these days. Yet they used to be here twice every Sunday.'

'Well, it's not surprising really – George is such a rigid disciplinarian at home, you know. Insists that the children do everything his way, and now they're older, they're just kicking over the traces. Can't say I blame them really.'

Being a parent is probably the toughest job that we will ever have to tackle, and the one for which we're likely to get the least support, and the most criticism. There's an awful lot of pressure put on us to be 'successful' or 'good' parents, by everyone from the grandparents to the health visitor, and a host of people in between. As a result, our children's behaviour is often seen as a measure of how we are doing as parents; 'bad' behaviour equals 'bad' parents. Whether we are seen as too lax or too strict, we tend to be held responsible for all our children do and get awarded brickbats or bouquets accordingly!

Naturally enough we prefer praise to blame, and do our best. But a tiny child is totally self-centred by nature, and demands instant gratification of all his needs. So the task of teaching him to accept boundaries to his behaviour and develop self-control to the point where he can wait for what he wants, and consider the needs of others, is a long and tricky one. However, it is not an optional extra, to be grappled with on the days when we feel up to it. We all need to live within boundaries, and discipline is simply the tool we use to help ourselves, and to teach our children, to stay within those boundaries.

When our children are tiny, our job is to look after them, keeping them warm, fed, safe and loved. At this stage the protective guidelines have to be imposed from the outside by parents, teachers, or other carers. But as children leave infancy behind, discipline will only be effective if it grows out of a loving relationship. It is still applied by the parents, but always with the aim of helping the child to develop the maturity necessary for self-discipline and responsibility for their own actions and attitudes.

As children grow up, discipline becomes more and more an inward thing, with us gradually relinquishing the role of caretaker and rule-enforcer, and hopefully ending up as friend and consultant. In the relatively short space of eighteen years, we change from being totally responsible for a baby, to being not responsible at all (at least in law) when they reach adulthood.

The way in which we discipline our children will vary with our parenting style. If we are authoritarian 'do-it-my-way' parents, we may see ourselves as 'doing it all for the children's good', but if our way is not followed, we quickly resort to shouting, smacking and random punishment to enforce our will. Children brought up under this kind of regime are likely to show one of three reactions: fight, flight, or submission.

A child who is a fighter doesn't necessarily resist an authoritarian adult outwardly, but often seethes with resentment inwardly, growing up with an unspoken determination to do their own thing as soon as they are physically able.

Children who resort to the 'flight' response don't literally run away (although they may do) but tend to melt into the background whenever adults are around. They are often reluctant to express a point of view, and raised voices or strongly held opinions terrify them. They tend to be withdrawn and find it very hard to make relationships.

A child who submits may do so out of fear, and because they have decided that, in the eyes of the adults they love, they don't count for much. They will then find it hard to establish their own sense of values and may easily become the victims of bullying at school. As adults, it will be very hard for them to have any sense of self-worth.

Permissive 'do-as-you-like' parents represent the other side of the parenting coin. Rather than having very rigid boundaries, they appear to have none at all, and interestingly enough, children find this excess freedom very hard to handle. They tend to become increasingly demanding, in an effort to provoke their parents into saying where the boundaries for acceptable behaviour do lie. They expect their needs to be met instantly, without giving any consideration to the needs of others, and often end up labelled 'spoilt', and thoroughly unpopular with adults and other children alike.

Both these styles of parenting show how we can use or abuse power within the family. Authoritarian parents hold all the power themselves; permissive parents hand it over to the children. As a result there is always one who tends to be the loser. But there is a third way. If we are willing to try the 'responsible' or power-sharing route, we will still be very clear about our responsibility to teach and train our children and take it very seriously. We will still have very definite boundaries for different ages and stages, and be tough about enforcing them when necessary. But it will not be done with any idea of winners or losers, but in a spirit of working together to see that both parents' and children's needs are met.

Why does he behave like this?

'I just don't know what gets into her!' I suspect that every parent has said that at one time or another, as they scoop up a furious toddler, or are given the 'silent treatment' by a resentful teenager. We might do better to ask 'What is trying to get out of her?' The Bible tells us that in the beginning human beings chose to turn from following God's way, and this bias is present in all of us from birth. In addition there are a certain number of basic needs that everybody shares. These are neither good nor bad in themselves – the problems come with the way we try to fulfil them. American psychologist Abraham Maslow describes them as forming a pyramid shape, which breaks down the two all-encompassing needs of security and significance into five layers.

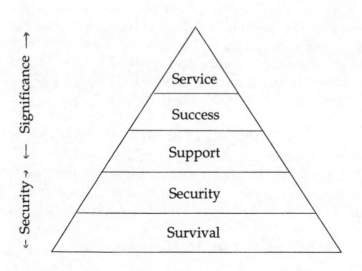

■ Survival
This covers our most basic physical needs: for food, shelter, warmth, sleep, etc.

■ Security
Once we are certain of staying alive, we look for enough money for comfort and relaxation, protection and structure to our lives.

■ Support
This could also be called 'loving and belonging'. We need to be loved and to love in return. We find this first in our families and then move out into friendship and other relationships.

■ Success
We need to be recognized and accepted for who we are; to be able to achieve things and to succeed in the tasks we set ourselves.

■ Service
Maslow calls this 'self-actualization', and sees it as our capacity to look beyond ourselves, striving for things like equality and justice, once we have had our basic needs met. I would see it as an all-important spiritual dimension: our commitment to others and to God which is both the baseline and the pinnacle of a truly fulfilled life.

Naughty or needy?

When my newborn grandson is hungry, he cries. When he is too hot, too cold or uncomfortable in other ways, he cries. At the moment he cries very little, and so tends to be dubbed a 'good' baby. Actually his behaviour is neither 'good' nor 'bad'. His survival needs are at stake, and so he lets us know about it in the only way he can. His parents know that, and wouldn't dream of calling him 'naughty' for crying – even when his wails disturb their much longed-for sleep!

At this stage it is easy to see how needs trigger behaviour, and how as parents we need to respond, but it gets more complicated as the child grows older. Within the family circle, it isn't just the children who have needs, parents have them too. It may sound very selfish to say that we need to care for our own needs, but if we feel exhausted physically, and battered emotionally, we have little to offer others. As the children grow older, we may find that we judge their behaviour by the way it affects us. If it stops us from meeting our own needs of the moment, then we see it as negative behaviour; if it doesn't interfere with our needs, we take a far more positive view.

A newborn baby who wants his mother's attention can do nothing other than cry. A toddler and older child has a far greater range of possibilities! Look at the following examples of behaviour to see what kind of needs you think the child might be expressing. Would they impose on a need that you might have in that situation? How do you think you might react? Would you see them as 'naughty' or 'needy'?

1. Two-year-old Darren insists on dressing himself, even though he takes ages and can't do up his buttons. He screams furiously when you try to help.
2. You have been chatting to a friend in the supermarket for half an hour, and Lucy, who is four, knocks a stack of tins all over the floor.
3. Robert spends all his pocket money buying sweets for his friends.
4. Naomi says she would rather not go to the disco at all than be collected by you at 10.30 p.m.

The way we react is likely to be influenced by how we are feeling, and what our needs are at the time. If we are tired, irritable or otherwise under pressure, we are far more likely to become annoyed than if we are in a happy frame of mind.

It will also be affected by who is doing it. A baby who kicks and splashes in the bath is likely to be applauded. Her schoolboy brothers who have a water fight are liable to be hauled out of the water, and told to clear up the mess.

Where and when the action takes place also makes a difference. I may enjoy my son's efforts to bowl a cricket ball accurately in the garden, but feel decidedly embarrassed when he practises his bowling action (without the ball) as we walk down the High Street!

How do we set boundaries to behaviour?

The boundaries which we set for our children will be largely influenced by our own personal values. Some parents will also want to consider the Bible's boundaries which we looked at earlier. In a nutshell they were:

- loving yourself and respecting your own needs
- loving others and respecting their needs
- loving and respecting God and his commandments.

■ Loving yourself and respecting your own needs

As we have already seen, a newborn baby can do nothing for itself, and its needs are those of survival, security and emotional support. All these things have to be provided by the parents. When the baby becomes a toddler, she will need to be protected from electric points, hot fires and a host of other threats to life and limb by physical restraint, if necessary, and to learn the meaning of the word 'no'. But in order to meet her needs to belong and succeed, her parents will also have to give her lots of hugs and cuddles as well as correction, and supervised freedom, so that she can learn to walk, run, jump and climb. She, and they, will gradually find out what she can and can't do. It's a learning process all round!

How far along the road to personal responsibility are your children? Can they:

- feed, dress and wash themselves
- go to bed and get up with minimum supervision
- get things ready for school
- choose suitable clothes to wear on a day-to-day basis
- accept responsibility for a chore and do it regularly
- get on with homework without reminders?

■ Loving others and respecting their needs

At first a child is completely self-centred, and he has to learn how to love and respect others, step by step, as he becomes more emotionally mature. This will mean considerable supervision of social relationships, for under-fives at least.

When our second son was a baby, two-year-old David 'shared' his metal Dinky cars by throwing them into the carry-cot with a gleeful 'Here y'are baby'. We didn't want to squash his generous instincts (if that is what they were!) but in order to allow Angus to survive infancy we had to borrow a cat net and a playpen! As the boys got a little older, they went through a phase of being reluctant to share their special toys with visiting friends, so we agreed to leave those in the cupboard when others were in the house, and have a box of 'sharing' toys, which were brought out only on those occasions.

What stage of 'social responsibility' are your children at? Are they able to:

- play with other children and share toys

- respect other people's possessions and accept that they must not be touched without permission
- allow adults to talk without interrupting
- talk politely to adults from outside the family
- choose their own friends and activities, but be reliable about letting you know where they are going and with whom?

This is obviously a random selection of possibilities, but shows how children progress gradually in the way that they can handle social situations.

■ Loving and respecting God and his commandments

A recent survey shows that the majority of parents hold honesty and reliability as key values that they would want their children to hold. And most of us would recognize the rightness and importance of respecting parents, not murdering, not slandering someone else, and refraining from adultery or wrecking another's marriage.

Parents who have a personal religious faith will obviously think it's important to have a spiritual dimension to family life. The family needs to share in prayer and worship and link with the wider community of faith. So what extras might a family focus on in order to build a specifically God-ward dimension to their family life? What practical steps can a family take towards:

- putting God and his standards first
- learning the basics of the faith
- worshipping with others
- celebrating the major festivals
- praying – as individuals and as a family?

In these areas especially, actions speak louder than words!

Checks and balances

It is good and helpful to have a clear picture of the values and standards of behaviour that we are trying to instill into our children, but the time will certainly come when they will push against the limits we have set, just to see if we mean what we say. Then what do we do? Before we had children, most of us will have watched other parents do battle with their children, often in the most embarrassingly public places, and vowed we would never resort to bribing, shouting, threatening and smacking – only to fail horribly when similarly tested! So is there a better way? There are at least four possibilities that have the virtue of being effective at least some of the time, with most children on many occasions! They are:

- talking things through
- learning from consequences
- the firm but gentle 'no'
- physical correction.

■ Talking things through

As with nations, so with families – if we can negotiate an agreed solution rather than resorting to verbal or physical 'fisticuffs', so much the better. Imagine the situation: you have just cleared up the kitchen and are looking forward to a quiet cup of coffee! Your daughter and two of her friends arrive and ask if they can do the baking they have promised to do for the Youth Club Shop. Last time they did this the kitchen looked like a disaster area afterwards. What do you do?

a) Remind them of the last episode and say no?
b) Agree, but keep rushing into the kitchen to see what they're doing?

c) Check that they have the ingredients that they need and say something like: 'I know that you need to get this cooking done, but I've spent a lot of time cleaning up the kitchen this afternoon, and I really need a sit down before Dad and I go out this evening. After the mess you made last time, I'm afraid that if I hand the kitchen over to you, I'll have a lot of extra clearing up to do and be late and fed up which will spoil our evening. How can we arrange things so that that doesn't happen?' (You could impose a solution, but if the girls make a commitment it's more likely that they'll do it cheerfully.) They may decide to go and do their cooking elsewhere, buy what they need from the supermarket, or promise to have the kitchen spick and span again within a given time.

What have you accomplished by handling the problem in this way? You have acknowledged that your daughter and her friends have a valid need, but also explained that you have a need that must be respected. Rather than raking up old grievances and accusing them of being thoughtless, careless or untidy, you have:

- described what you see as the problem
- told them what effect that has had on you
- told them how you feel about that
- asked for their help in solving the problem.

■ Learning from consequences

If we want to have children who take responsibility for their own behaviour, rather than being goaded into action by punishments or rewards, we need to allow them, wherever possible, to make their own decisions and then live with the consequences of their actions. You obviously wouldn't take this route if it would bring them into real danger – for example, a toddler shouldn't ride his bike on the road; it would be very unwise to allow a young teenager to walk home alone after dark in most areas; certain sorts of videos and films hold real moral danger for our children. But if your daughter spends all her pocket money on make-up as soon as she gets it, she can go without sweets or comics – until the next 'pay day'. If your trendy son insists on going to school in winter without his sweater or coat, he will feel cold.

We can also use this method of living with consequences when we have a rather larger cause of conflict. Imagine the scene: Jenny, aged eight, and ten-year-old Michael are watching television, and Michael gets bored with the programme that his sister is enjoying. He has possession of the remote control switch, and so flicks over on to another channel. She asks him to turn back to the original programme and, when he refuses, tries to grab the remote control. A battle royal then ensues. What can you do?

a) Rush in and separate them, giving them both a smack?
b) Confiscate the remote control?
c) Turn the television off, and say something like: 'If you carry on like this, the television or the remote control will get broken. If you want to watch TV you must either agree on a programme that you both want to watch, or decide that one of you chooses today and the other one chooses tomorrow. Either way, neither of you holds the remote control; it stays on top of the TV. If you can't decide what to do, we will turn the television off for this evening, and you can try again tomorrow.'

Simply saying 'no'

Some children are naggers, who wear their parents down with whining and refusing to accept that they can't have or do something that they want. They are also quick to play one parent off against the other, going to one and then to the other for an alternative decision. This is where a policy of backing one another's decisions in public (even though we may disagree in private) is very helpful.

Some of us find it difficult to say 'no', perhaps because we haven't worked out clear guidelines for a given area of behaviour and we wonder whether we are being unfair or unreasonably strict. A child soon senses when we are uncertain, and is usually quick to exploit the situation. However, once we have made a decision we can confidently give our child a brief explanation and, if the request is repeated, simply answer 'no'. This is a particularly useful ploy at the supermarket checkout!

Johnny: Can I have some sweets please?
Mother: Not today darling. You've got enough at
           home.
Johnny: I want some.
Mother: No.
Johnny: *(whining)* I don't like my sweets at home.
Mother: *(softly)* No.
Johnny: *(yelling)* I want some sweets.
Mother: *(even more softly)* No.

The key to using 'no' without resorting to shouting, arguing or feeling like a monster is:

- you have thought about why you are saying 'no' and feel that that is the right approach for this occasion
- because you are confident, you stay relaxed and calm
- having given your reason, you refuse to be drawn into an argument
- you resist the temptation to try and out-shout your child, and keep your 'no' firm but soft and gentle.

With teenagers it's often helpful to ask for notice of requests that require some thought, like extensions to curfew times and invitations to parties. This allows you to think about your response, and talk it over with your partner before giving your answer. It's hard to make a reasoned decision when you are rung up from the Youth Club with a 'Can I stay at Mandy's tonight? Hurry up, Mum, I've only got ten pence!'

Sometimes it is right for a child to say 'no' and in our efforts to teach them respect for adults, they need to know that. There may be an occasion when we ask a child to take on a responsibility for which they don't feel ready; in this situation it is right for them to say no. Sadly many children have been sexually abused because they haven't realized that it is right to say 'no' when they are touched in a way that they don't like. We need to reassure our children that if they have a reason for saying 'no' we are willing to listen.

Spare the rod?

Although the whole point of discipline is to work with the child, so that boundaries to behaviour are accepted and infringements are few, there are bound to be occasions when the subject of punishment rears its ugly head. There are four main ways in which we tend to punish misbehaviour:

- restitution – putting damage right by paying towards the cost, either in cash or by working
- withdrawal of privileges – which might be anything from missing a favourite television programme to having to stay at home rather than going out with friends
- exclusion – being sent out of the room until the child can behave in a socially acceptable way
- corporal punishment.

There's usually little discussion about whether the first three methods are acceptable – as long as the punishment fits the crime, there's no real problem. But the subject of corporal punishment is one that is hotly debated today. One camp blames its abolition in schools for almost all the nation's ills, while those of the opposite viewpoint equate a spanking with child abuse. Some believe very strongly that when the Bible mentions discipline, it means physical correction. Others feel that just as we no longer stone adulterers, rapists or rebellious young men, the emphasis on beating and other forms of physical punishment as the means of discipline in some parts of the Old Testament is largely cultural. The Bible rightly says that a *loving* father instructs and disciplines his child, but today (many argue) the nature of that discipline may be different to that given in Old Testament times.

All parents have carefully to decide on the rights and wrongs of corporal punishment for themselves. These pointers may help in that decision:

1. Some children respond better to an immediate spank than a long 'telling off'. Our youngest son, who hated long discussions, said once after being scolded, 'You batter me with words.'
2. If used at all, it is probably best to use spanking rarely and only to correct deliberate and wilful disobedience.
3. If a parent is frequently spanking a child who is older than seven or eight, there is something amiss with the discipline/self-discipline process and outside help should be sought.
4. Corporal punishment is no longer allowed in schools and is totally forbidden in some European countries.

Before any form of punishment is used a child should be:

- reminded of the boundaries and the reason for them
- told what will happen if they continue with their bad behaviour.

When the punishment has been given (especially if it is a spanking) mop up their tears, comfort them, and reassure them of your love.

Don't punish in anger. If you're seething with frustration and fury send your child into another room, or leave the room yourself, until you can think more coolly and calmly about the situation.

And finally... parents are people too. However hard we try, there are bound to be times when we fail in our attempts to discipline our children in the right way, and for their good. So when we make mistakes and discipline unfairly or unreasonably, we too need to say 'I'm sorry – please forgive me.' It won't undermine our authority; it will amaze and humble us to discover what loving and forgiving people our children can be.

6
Surviving the Deluge

'But God remembered Noah and all the wild animals and the livestock that were with him in the ark.'

When we got engaged, the pressure cooker was the kitchen gadget of the moment. 'You must have one!' a newly married friend urged as she surveyed our wedding present list. 'Mince, onions, potatoes, carrots – into the pressure cooker after church, and that's your Sunday lunch done in minutes!' Gordon blanched at the thought of this alternative to a Sunday roast and flatly refused to ask for a gadget with such potential to destroy his comfort. I didn't argue. I was secretly terrified of the hissing, steaming monster, and convinced that it would blow up in my face at the slightest provocation.

Family life is rather like a pressure cooker. In a family you have a group of people at different stages of maturity, all consciously or unconsciously seeking to fulfil those basic human needs for security and significance. Think back to Abraham Maslow's pyramid. It reminds me of the baskets inside the metal pressure cooker container, all fitting together and pressing against one another. Add some 'heat' in the form of:

- problems within myself
- problems caused by others in my immediate circle
- problems from the world around
- problems in my relationship with God

... and watch that head of steam build up!

What fuels the pressure?

Look back over your life in the past twelve months. What kinds of pressure have you experienced?

■ Within yourself

Have you experienced illness, new ways of thinking, guilt over some particular problem, disturbing memories, changes in the way you see or understand yourself, lack of love or appreciation...?

■ Within your immediate family circle

Have you had a bereavement, a new baby, extra care for an elderly relative, children entering their teens or leaving home, problems with money, started a new job or lost one...?

■ Problems from the world around

Have you taken on a new responsibility at work, at church, or within the community? Have you had a new boss, or different colleagues? Are your new neighbours noisy, your old ones quarrelsome, or is the area where you live going through changes for better or worse...?

■ Problems in your relationship with God

St Augustine wrote: 'Thou hast created us for Thyself, and our heart is not quiet until it rests in Thee.' In recognizing God's total love and acceptance we can take a vital step towards emotional and spiritual health; in rejecting God's way for our life we can bring upon ourselves guilt and unhappiness.

So why have any of those events or experiences seemed particularly difficult to handle? Did they threaten your survival needs, your security or support needs, your opportunities to succeed or achieve, or interfere with your spiritual life in some way?

The thing that creates the pressure is not necessarily the situation itself but our reaction to it. Moving house is supposed to be a very stressful event, but when I was a child, we moved every two or three years because of my father's job. My parents appeared to accept this quite cheerfully, and so I did too. Then I got married to a dentist who, having bought a practice in a market town, had every expectation of staying put for the course of his working life. Not having any prospect of moving was initially a real stress factor for me!

Sometimes we find life unbearably stressful because we take on problems and burdens that are not really ours to carry. Have another think about the pressures you have experienced recently. Were they all actually your problems, or something that really affected another family member?

When he was sixteen, Jonathon was unsure about what long-term plans he wanted to make for his life, and so he was persuaded to stay on at school and apply to go to college. When his school exam results came out, he hadn't achieved the grades that he needed. He was quite cheerful about it because he was secretly relieved to get away from formal education for a while. His father saw it as a catastrophe! The event was the same: Jonathon didn't achieve the right exam results to enable him to go to college. Why were their reactions so different?

Jonathon's view of the event	His father's view
He was unconcerned, because he didn't see higher education as vital to his success in life.	His father saw it as a disaster, because he put a very high value on formal qualifications and job success.

Jonathon's feelings	His father's feelings
He felt relief and a sense of freedom.	He experienced great anxiety and concern for what his son would do next.

Although we can make our lives more difficult by taking on board responsibilities that are not ours, the very fact of living in a community has an unavoidable effect on us. John Donne said that 'no man is an island' and this is certainly true in family relationships. One person's problems do have a knock-on effect upon the rest of the group.

Imagine what life would have been like in the last year, if your partner had had back trouble, and as a result was forced to change to a different job which offered no overtime. This made meeting the winter bills a problem. In addition to this he has missed his old friends at work, and in his spare time can no longer play in the local football team. The new job doesn't give him as much satisfaction as the previous one, and his back pain makes it difficult for him to play with the children at the weekends. It's a difficult time, but you're coping – just. However, if you are experiencing difficulties of your own, in one or more areas of your life, and perhaps your children are also having a tough time, it is easy to see how quickly life can seem to become unmanageable.

Have a look at your whole family's 'pressure gauge'. You might like to fill it in together. When you see how each one has been feeling, it may give you fresh insight into why things have been a little hard going recently, or relatively plain sailing.

OUR FAMILY'S PRESSURE GAUGE

	My Partner	Child (1)	Child (2)	Child (3)
Me				
Service				
Success				
Support				
Security				
Survival				

Spiritual

Psychological
Mental

Social
∧
Emotional

Physical

← Significance → ← Security →

Change points

Although the patterns of family life are constantly changing as children and parents grow and develop, there are certain 'transition' points where we particularly notice the pressure. These are times when the structure of our lives is significantly altered by a new member of the family joining us, or an older one leaving. We may have a new job, a new home, a new school or new friends, and while there may be pleasure at the 'new' things, there's inevitably an element of grieving over the loss of the 'old' things, situations and relationships. We often feel very tired and, if the transition isn't one that we welcome, we may experience other physical symptoms of distress like stomach upsets or aches and pains that have no obvious cause. It takes time to adapt and accept the new situation, and it's quite normal to feel insecure and uncomfortable until we adjust to the new rhythms that these changes bring with them.

Four years ago, our second son went to live and study in the United States for a year. Two weeks after he left, a ten-year-old came to live with us for several months. As our older three children were now all living away from home on a day-to-day basis, our younger daughter had to get used to being the middle child of three, instead of the youngest of five. It was hard going for her. Shortly after Gemma's arrival, our eldest son was ill and returned home to convalesce for several weeks. His fiancée, with whom he was planning a summer wedding, naturally spent all her free time at our house too! As wedding preparations went on apace, friends called and the walls of the house bulged, my mother-in-law experienced a marked deterioration of an ongoing problem with her sight, and I discovered a mysterious lump in my leg which the doctor refused to ignore on the grounds that 'it's probably nothing but...' Just like a toy kaleidoscope, the pattern of our days was constantly reforming, as one transition followed another.

1989 was a hot and weary summer both inside and outside of our house!

_____ **Parents in pain** _____

The Bible is full of stories of families who had rebellious children; it is a problem that is as old as time itself. And although a degree of rebellion and wanting to think things through for themselves is not only natural but a normal part of healthy growth, there is great pain for parents whose children appear totally and deliberately to reject the values that they hold very dear.

First of all, there is the huge sense of waste and sadness if we see our children's bright potential apparently lost as they play truant or fritter away their time at school, gang up with friends who shoplift, flirt with drugs or in other ways flout the law, or maybe have to face teenage pregnancy or other long-term life-changing decisions.

Then there's a great tendency to blame ourselves, to ask 'What did we do wrong?' and for marriages to be put under considerable pressure if one parent wants to handle the situation in one way, and the other parent sees the issues differently. Sadly, Christians often find it even more difficult than those for whom church going is not such an intrinsic part of life when they have to admit that they're finding it very hard to handle their problems, and to ask for help and support. So often the church has very high standards for family life in theory, and tends to deny the possibility that loving and conscientious parents can ever have erring children. For this reason, when it happens, the sense of failure tends to be greater, and the fear of criticism and judgement rather than love and support makes it more difficult to ask for help. The pain of this particular situation goes very deep and is extremely difficult to bear.

Although, for most of us, family life is a positive experience overall, when the pressure is on, it can seem as if we do more crying than celebrating. But, as a wise counsellor friend once said, 'The pearl is the autobiography of the oyster'. That little bit of sand which is such an irritant in the oyster shell can be turned into something beautiful and life changing if we will work with it instead of fighting against it.

Our older three children bobbed through adolescence with a few choppy patches, but it wasn't until number four hit thirteen that we had any idea what the 'turbulent teens' really meant. Because our children are widely spread in age, this period coincided with older children leaving home, our own parents ageing, two of them dying, and the ordinary pressures of mid-life, which can seem very testing at the time. Desperately we prayed and searched for some way of coping, talking to friends who had weathered similar storms before us. We eventually came to the conclusion that, although there are no pat answers which will automatically pour oil on troubled waters, there are certain principles which, if applied judiciously, can help to keep us afloat when the waves of pressure threaten to swamp us.

SURVIVAL STRATEGIES

Recognize: walk alertly

■ **The time for change**

'You're miles behind the times – things are different now!' How often parents hear that from their children! And although we may not be quite as out of touch with life as our children like to think, we are often slow to recognize that we have reached a time for change in our pattern of living.

When our older children were small, one of the ways in which we chose to make Sunday a different day was to do something special with them in the afternoon. Each member of the family took it in turns to decide what we did, and whatever it was, we did it together rather than the children 'going out to play' as they often did at other times. All went well until David was approaching his teens. He then began to want to spend time with his friends on a Sunday. At first this seemed really disruptive, because it 'spoiled' the very pleasant tradition we had established and which the younger ones still enjoyed. There was a lot more tension than harmony in our Sundays until we woke up to the fact that a time for change had come. We had to accept that, and begin to create new patterns that were right for the situation as it was now, and not as it had been.

■ Who needs change?

'You are ultimately responsible for your own life journey, and the only person that you can decide to change, with God's help, is yourself.' When I was first confronted with that idea, I felt as if a huge load had been lifted off my shoulders. I wanted to believe it but it went against everything that I had previously been taught. I was firmly of the opinion that as a 'caring Christian', not only was I responsible for myself, but the rest of the world as well! Not surprisingly, I wasn't coping.

When we are facing a difficult situation as parents, it's easy to be so absorbed in the problem that we completely fail to recognize that we can't force our partners or children to change, or make them respond in the way that we want them to. Of course we want to support and care for them, and meet their needs to the best of our ability, and we can make it easier for them to change by the way we act and react. But we can only give to them if our own 'batteries' of spiritual and emotional resources and physical energy have been charged. So at a pressurised time we need to ask ourselves:

- what are my needs now?
- what practical steps do I need to take to meet those needs?
- how does God want to change me and my reactions?

When Jesus told the man in the Gospel to 'love your neighbour as yourself' he appears to be assuming that his questioner would love himself as a matter of course. Many people today, however, seem to have low self-esteem, and actually have to have permission to 'love themselves'. We need to remind ourselves constantly that if God loves and accepts us just as we are, we can do the same, with humility and realism. Then we can take steps to meet our own needs without fearing that we are being self-centred or complacent.

One of the most powerful and important resources that we can draw on to recharge our batteries in a time of pressure is that of pouring out all our concerns to God in prayer. He is the perfect listener, who never tires of hearing us confess our failures or rehearse the same problems over and over again. We need no set time or place, no 'religious' form of words or style. And we can trust him to give us insights into what we need to do when we spend time with him – either as we read the Bible, or as we sit quietly and simply listen for the prompting of his Spirit in our hearts and minds.

■ How can I change?
It is very hard to change the ingrained habits of many years, but God can (if we let him!) not only make us aware of areas

where we need to change our attitudes or behaviour, but also give us the grace and ability to do so, little by little.

Release – walk free

It's a great step when we recognize that we don't have to carry the burdens of the entire family. And we can take a further step towards freedom when we realize that even the responsibilities that are ours can be shared with God.

There's the well-known saying, 'a problem shared is a problem halved'. Yet our relationship with God can be more than a source of emotional comfort! God, as our heavenly Father, is able to join with us in meeting the parenting responsibilities we face. 'Give us today our daily bread', we pray – but our needs as parents may not be for physical food with which to feed our family but for solutions to our children's problems in growing up and gaining independence. Alongside our cries of worry can be prayers that ask God to solve what to us looks intractable or beyond our control.

Sometimes we have the privilege of seeing how we can be part of God's solution to a problem straight away, but often we have to release the whole thing completely to him first, and trust him to deal with it. Then he will either involve us in helping to work things out, or deal with it in a way that we have no part in.

I find it helpful to imagine that I am putting my problem into a basket and placing it in God's hands. Sometimes it is the kind that often floats over our garden in the summer, attached to a hot air balloon. If that gas-filled balloon is released from its moorings with something in the basket (other than a pilot!) it will simply float out of sight, taken by the wind and air currents, no longer my responsibility and certainly completely out of my control.

We are more often asked to play our part, knowing that it is insufficient in itself. I remember school plays many years ago. Mine was never a big part: I was Osric the messenger, never Hamlet. Yet my small part *was* needed. And so with parenting. As I fulfil my responsibilities, God directs the action on the broader stage.

_____ Relax: walk gently _____

Many parents have great dreams for their children, imagining that they'll follow in their parents' footsteps, carrying on a family tradition in work or sport, or do something quite different and fulfil hopes that the parents were not able to bring about in their own lives. This may happen, but more often children have their own gifts and ambitions, and struggling to ram a square peg into a round hole is very stressful for both parties. Our job is not to force them into our mould, but relax, accept what is important to them, and gently create the very best conditions that we can for the flowering of their own talents.

We may also need to learn to be gentle with ourselves. Many of us have a little tape recorder inside our head which chatters on endlessly about what we should do, have failed to do, or could have done better! At the end of a difficult day it can be rather like being a prisoner in the dock, faced with a very ferocious prosecuting counsel!

Of course we do make mistakes, and occasionally they do have far-reaching effects, which have to be recognized, put right as far as we are able and the consequences lived through. But the guilt that most of us batter ourselves with is the false guilt of perfectionism. Few of us would ever deliberately do things that hurt those we love, and most of our parenting is a matter of doing the very best that we know how to do at the time. If we can honestly say that, and are prepared both to learn from our mistakes and develop our skills as much as we are able, then we can come to God and to our children for forgiveness when we know we have fallen short, and walk free of guilt.

This is important because if we listen to that negative tape, we are likely to become defeated and discouraged. And what is worse, we are likely to act out all those negative things. Remember what we said about labels becoming self-fulfilling? So we need to become our own defence lawyers, reminding ourselves when necessary that God has both forgiven and forgotten. We can then re-run the tapes with positive messages, focusing on our successes, and giving ourselves permission to enjoy them.

When I am feeling 'frayed at the edges' I often read Psalm 37, where we are told five times in the first eight verses to 'trust' God and not to 'fret'. So often we make a vague attempt to bring our worries to God, but instead of leaving them with him, by an act of our will we pick them up and take them home with us again! Trust is like a muscle – the harder we work it, the stronger it grows.

Rejoice: walk singing

'The Lord will make us equal to the task.'

This encouraging statement is carved round a huge modern candlestick in Lincoln Cathedral. I think it should be emblazoned on a banner and handed to every parent who is feeling beleaguered and whose confidence is beginning to sag.

Imagine that you are applying to be the parent of your particular child. First, write down all the things that you love about your child: these are the reasons why you want this particular job! Then write down all the things you feel he or she needs in a parent. What positive skills and experiences do you have to offer so that these needs can be met? It may be anything from 'I make lovely jam tarts' to 'I'm good at soothing teachers with fierce voices'. Aim for at least ten items to start with, and try to add to it regularly. Keep it where you can see it, and read it aloud occasionally when the pressure begins to build up. Don't let negative thoughts and feelings blind you to how well you are doing. Remind yourself that you're the successful applicant for this post!

And when feelings of inadequacy creep up, remember the candlestick in Lincoln Cathedral. If God has entrusted you with children, he can be relied on to give you all the resources you need to do a great job!

7

Happy Landings

'At the end of the hundred and fifty days the water had gone down, and... the ark came to rest on the mountains.'

Once upon a time, a young man and his bride set out upon the journey of family life. They were accompanied to the boatyard by their elders, who gave them much good advice, and not a little material with which they could build the ship in which they were to set sail. Much daunted by the task ahead of them the couple considered well the plans which had been used to shape their parents' boats, and both began to build.

Boat building was more difficult than they had bargained for, and after many days, the couple were discouraged. 'This hull is both too clumsy and unsightly,' declared the woman. 'It will but labour through the water if it should move at all. My needs will be much better met by a more graceful vessel – a boat to skim across the waves with lightness and with speed.'

'What foolish words are these!' exclaimed her husband. ''Tis better far to stay afloat than risk our all for speed. This structure's served my family well through six generations. We will build according to this plan.'

At this the wife was much displeased, and foreswore further labour, claiming that her husband was tied to his mother's apron strings and cared more for his family's approval than for her needs. The man named irresponsibility and stubbornness as two of her vices, and turned to consult the other couples and the one or two solitary boat builders, who were toiling beside them. But they had little help to give, for all had conflicting views upon the matter.

Dark clouds began to gather, and it seemed possible that the boat would not be built but rather that each would seek another partner with whom to create a vessel more to their individual liking. Happily, before this state of affairs could come to pass, the Master builder came to call upon the yard. Seeing that the man and woman were given more to destroying the other's work than they were to encouraging one another's efforts, he invited them into his workshop. There he bade them view the racks of plans for boats of many sizes and designs that lined the walls.

'Each one,' he said, 'is freshly drawn to meet the needs of those who sail within it. You too must find the unique style of ship to carry you upon the journey that you alone will take. Study with care the base design that I will give you. Learn much from those who went before you, but mark their errors and consider well your needs.' With this advice, the man and woman embarked upon their labours with renewed zest and courage, and soon their boat was ready to set out upon its voyage.

As they journeyed on, children were added to their company, and as each child was born, the fabric of the boat had to be reshaped a little so that the needs of all on board were met.

Sometimes the days were sunny and the journey seemed all joy. Parents and children played together and worked in harmony, and the fleet with which they sailed pressed close around them, and gave them strength and courage.

But oftentimes the man and his wife were much wearied. They laboured alone, and saw little obvious fruit for their toil. The children grumbled at the tasks they had entrusted to them, and when the storms whipped up the waves so that the boat shivered and creaked, all they could do was lash themselves and their offspring to the mast, as the Master builder had shown them, and pray for morning.

At last the day came when the children wanted their own boats. To start with they were well content with the small craft that their parents had ready for them, which bobbed along in the wake of the larger vessel – guided and fuelled by their parents' hand. The man and the woman congratulated themselves upon their forward thinking and hoped that life would always be this way. But alas, all too soon the moment arrived when the tethering rope was cut, and the children prepared to set out on their own journeys. 'Their boats are too small,' wept the woman, 'and the modifications that they have made do not please me. When they sail out of sight, how will they fare if they heed not our instructions? And who will come to our aid, when this ship of ours needs mending and we are too old to labour as before?'

'They have had many years in which to observe our skills and profit from our mistakes,' replied the man. 'We have given them a map and compass and bread for the journey, and have told them where to find the Master builder for themselves. They have a task to fulfil for which we have equipped them with all the wisdom we possess. Beyond that we cannot go. Love will bring them to our aid should we require it, and love will tune our ears to hear their call. Come, let us trim our sails, for there is much for us to do still, and many joys ahead. Call not this parting of the ways the beginning of life's ending, but rather say it is but the end of its beginning.'